OVERCOMING

FEAR

An Essential Guide for The Audacious Young Adult
By Prince Aryee

Prince Aryee

Overcoming Fear - An Essential Guide for The
Audacious Young Adult
Registration No: 1180913

Canadian Intellectual Property Office | An
Agency of Industry Canada
© 2021 Prince Aryee
www.mindsovercomingfear.com

Published by: Prince Aryee

Cover Design by: Rose Graphix

Author Photo by: Maple Star Photography

ENDORSEMENT

"Prince does not write this from a place of wanton ignorance and theoretical wishful thinking. He has written a masterpiece, typifying his lived experiences. This book embodies his process and progress as he pursued God, the very one who has called us to eschew fear and live in Power, Love and soundness of mind. This book will transform your mindset, and, in the process, you'll find the courage to pursue your purpose"

Solomon Antwi

PRAYER

Dear Father,

Thank you for the gift of life.
Thank you for consistently being
active in my life.

I know fear isn't something that
you planted in me. That's exactly
why I want to start this journey
with you. Sometimes it seems like
I try to handle things on my own
without acknowledging you.

This time, I'm asking you to be
at the centre of everything that I
do. Lord I come to you with all
the fear and anxiety that the devil
has placed in me.

I'm humbly asking you to help
me through it all and wipe any
distorted lens in my life so that I
can see you clearly and live a life
of freedom.

You are a good father and because of that, I know you have already started your work in me. Thank you for being by my side every day.

Amen.

"Never trust your fears. They don't know your strengths"
– Athena Singh

DEDICATION

To my father,

Many authors have made it a trend to thank famous people for motivation, but I want to honour you for all that you have done for me and for all the knowledge you have poured in me since I was a child.

I didn't understand a lot of things when I was younger. I misjudged many of your words and put my own meaning to your words of wisdom. Growing up, I've come to realize that those words shaped and moulded me to be the man that I am today.

I am more than grateful. I strongly believe that you were with me as I was writing this book simply because I would always hear your voice in my head repeating things that you said to me in the past. Thank you, dad, for being you.

Your son,

Prince

"You will never truly be free until you're living in authenticity"
– Christy Ann Martine

TABLE OF CONTENTS

"Everything you want is on the other side of fear"
– Jake Canfield

PREFACE

Fear is something I battled a lot growing up. My fear came in different forms, fear of rejection, fear of fear of separation, social anxiety and many more. I had to remind myself that regardless of how I feel the sun will always come up in the morning and the moon at night. So why would I let fear stop me from moving forward while the sun is still up there? Young adults in today's day and age have been represented in such a negative light. We are seen as people who aren't ambitious, people who want easy money and people who are less likely to go after their dreams.

However, many of these "judges" fail to look beyond the current mental state of young adults. Many of us have been through different challenges and obstacles that have shaped our minds or forced us to only run towards the safest option and we do so because our physical, mental and psychological wellbeing is under attack.

COVID-19 really opened my eyes to see that having a cure for a virus is the only way to freedom. Unfortunately, fear is one thing that you can't cure with physical medication. Your mind is the most powerful ground in your entire body. Once fear gets the chance to creep in, it creates its own living space where it dwells and controls your whole life. We all make mistakes, just learn from it, shake it off and keep pushing.

My whole purpose of writing this book is to help you navigate through your fears, face them like a soldier and leave with the keys to your freedom. Every chapter is full of knowledge and real-life experiences that will help you all through the journey of defeating FEAR.

Always keep in mind that I am with you through every step of the way. Stay focused and keep pushing. You

are one step away from kicking fear in
the b***.

"Courage doesn't always roar.
Sometimes courage is the little voice
at the end of the day that says:

I will try again tomorrow"

– Mary Radmacher

OVERCOMING

FEAR

Prince Aryee

FEAR

CHAPTER ONE

Fear to me is simply a mental state of uncertainty with a hint of danger and anxiety. As a young adult, fear is something that I battled a lot through schooling, working, and even personal experiences. I realized that the experiences that we go through as young adults shape our minds and hearts to submit to fear, but the good news is that "God hasn't given us the spirit of fear, but of power, and love, and of sound mind" – 2 Timothy 1:7. With negative opinions, pressure from society, and unexpected events like Covid-19, it's not a shock to me that young adults struggle with fear. There are so many types of fear in this world. Some include fear of heights, fear of flying, fear of thunder and lightning, fear of being alone and many more. One thing I want you to keep in mind is that It's okay to be scared, worried, insecure and unsure because when that happens, it's often a sign that you are about to take a bold step. We will specifically be targeting the fear that kills your vision, steals your joy and destroys your destiny.

Joshua 1:9 says that "This is my command. Be strong and courageous. Do not be afraid.

For the Lord your God is with you wherever you go". When you wake up every morning, is fear the first thing on your mind? Do you have doubts and regrets? If you have read this far it's a sign that you are one step away from your deliverance. This book was written to help you navigate through your challenges and obstacles. It was also written for people who are thinking about giving up because fear has captured their minds and people who believe that they are on earth to fulfill their purpose but are being slowed down by fear. It's time to take charge of your life and your mind and I strongly believe that your mindset will be renewed after reading this book.

Challenges and obstacles are all part of the journey of owning your identity. Many times, people think that challenges are the same as obstacles. They may feel the same but are not the same. Challenges are like exams or tests that we normally take in school. The only difference is that this test doesn't tell you when and how you will be taking it. Would your life be as interesting in the absence of obstacles?

Life challenges are there to force you to apply knowledge and wisdom that you have acquired in your years of living to real-life experiences. Obstacles, on the other hand, are like "speedbumps". They will always show up on your road to slow you down and potentially stop you from achieving greatness but with the right push and speed, you can overcome any barrier that's been placed ahead of you. Life will always throw curveballs at you, if you are lucky enough, you will escape it but if you fall because of the hit, you then have a choice to make. Will you stay down and accept defeat, or will you rise to your feet and try again? Now I do understand that some obstacles weren't placed by you and sometimes it's hard to acknowledge them and you might not even know how to erase them from your life but those are things that you need to work harder on to overcome. Build and change generational curses.

As a young adult, challenges and obstacles haven't been exempted from me. I face them daily, but I always have to remind myself that the mind is the battlefield for these problems. Luckily, I ultimately have the power and keys to lock and unlock any door that is either open or closed. With that in mind, I challenge myself to keep my mind in a state that won't cave into the hurdles of this world but rather press towards stability both in my mind and in my life. I was reading an article online and I came across a quote by Jimmy Dean that said, "I can't change the direction of the wind, but I can adjust my sails to always reach my destination". This quote constantly reminded me that the only person that can decide on which way to turn his sail is me. When you give up this power and allow the world to dictate things for you, you have placed the keys in the hands-on your biggest enemy. The sun shines in the morning and the moon shines in the night. If you are reading this book, I'm more than convinced that you know how these two things differ. That's exactly how life is. We are all unique in our ways and our challenges and obstacles will never be the same but that's the beauty of it. Never use the rubric of your neighbors' hurdles to evaluate the challenges and obstacles you face.

CONSEQUENCES OF NOT FACING YOUR FEAR

SELF DESTRUCTION

It's sad that many people lack knowledge on this topic and treat it as a joke. It can go as far as people thinking that "you are being extra" when you share your struggles; forgetting that mental health is a real thing. Your mental health includes your emotional, psychological, and social well-being. When you fail to see the importance of these things, you're at risk of losing control of your feelings, how you think and how you act.

"Be careful of how you think; your
life is shaped by your thoughts."
– Proverbs 4:23

THE BATTLES

Fears do not automatically leave after a month, a year, or even 10 years. Challenges and obstacles get tougher as time goes by. Running away from your fears comes at a cost that I do not think you are ready to pay. It's better to just face it and overcome it instead of pushing it aside; hoping that things will get better eventually. As a young adult, I struggled with the fear of emotional pain. I pride myself on being one of the most positive people in every setting, but this hurdle made me think twice and it made me feel like I was not being my true self. The mistake I made was that I allowed my past experiences to shape my thoughts. Trusting people became a challenge for me alongside opening up to people who genuinely cared about me. That is one of the challenges I faced all because I failed to step up, be a man, and face my fears. What price did you have to pay for not facing your fears?

Avoiding your fears can also be dangerous. You might feel better for a short period, but I want you to keep in mind that new problems and challenges can be generated, and you also put your mind at risk of losing its freedom.

"Nothing is more terrifying than battling your mind every single day."
-Anonymous

FEAR: THE CATALYST FOR FAILURE

I remember taking a quiz one morning in my 10th grade chemistry class. All I had to do was to write down the meaning of the word "catalyst". Luckily for me, I already studied the night before so writing it out was a breeze. As I was thinking about my experiences and challenges, I have faced in life, this word came running back to me. A catalyst is a substance that speeds up the rate of a chemical reaction without itself being consumed. Fear as a catalyst speeds up your rate of failure, disappointment and unwanted struggles without you even realizing it. It does it in such a smooth way that by the time you come to your senses, you have destroyed many things in your life and if you're not lucky, it will take divine intervention to save you! You have the ultimate power to decide if your life will be shaped by what people have told you, what you have heard or what you have seen, or you will take charge of your life and let the positive things shape your life. Not saying that failure can't shape you in a positive way, but you have to adopt the mindset that whatever happened to you came to serve a purpose. The lesson from your challenges on the other hand is yours to discover.

"Don't be embarrassed by your failures. Learn from them and start again."
-Anonymous

*"Fear is the path to the Dark Side.
Fear leads to anger, anger leads to
hate, hate leads to suffering."*
– Yoda

WHAT HAVE YOU LEARNED FROM THIS CHAPTER?

WHAT STEPS ARE YOU GOING TO TAKE TO BENEFIT FROM THE LESSON IN THIS CHAPTER?

CHAPTER TWO

How To Face Your Fears

As unhealthy as fears can be, I've realized that fears can be a good thing. You are probably asking yourself, "How can fear be a good thing?". Fear makes you more aware of bad things around you and increases the intensity of all your 5 senses. This in return makes your brain work more powerfully. You also have to keep in mind that fear can also stop you from making positive moves. There are lots of avenues that can be used to face fear, but this is what worked for me and I believe that it will work for you.

RECOGNIZING & ACCEPTING

The first step you have to take is to accept your flaws. Many people skip this step thinking that freedom can be attained without it. I always tell young adults around me that superior self-love cannot be built without going through the process of accepting your shortcomings. Failing to acknowledge your flaws can potentially lead to self-destruction. Life is also full of twists and turns. You will have good days and bad days, and it's important to understand that it's normal. Always remember that a perfect man doesn't exist, but the goal is to strive to "be the best that you can be".

"Once you have accepted your flaws, no one can use them against you."
– George R. R. Martin

It's important to know, accept and love your flaws because you can't defeat fear if you don't even know what you're facing. Liberation comes when self-realization takes place.

KILL YOUR IMAGINATIONS

Imaginations take you anywhere and anything you can imagine is real. Your thoughts carry a rare power to either make you prosper or make you suffer. When I say, "kill your imagination", I mean to kill any negative imagination that forces you to think less of yourself and encourages you to see the evil side of everything. But nurture the positive side that shows you all the delightful things on this earth.

"We suffer more often in imagination than in reality."

– Seneca

It is important to have a clear vision of how you want your life to be in the near future, "unless going with the flow" is something that you live by, which I believe is nonsense. Don't allow the wind of the earth to blow you in any direction that isn't geared towards the destination that you have defined for yourself.

TAKE CHARGE OF YOUR MIND

"The sky is not the limit. Your mind is."

– Lynette Simeone

In the first chapter, I talked about how powerful the mind is. This section, on the other hand, was written to help you "take charge of your mind". Many of us give up after failing the first time but it is in failing that success prevails. The mind is wired to make certain decisions based on things that you feel, see and smell. However, we have the power to overturn these decisions by adjusting to the mirrors that we choose to see ourselves in. The soul is made up of the mind, the emotion and the will. The mind is the ground for understanding, the emotion leads you to make rational or irrational decisions and the will determines what step you take. The main purpose of slavery is to take away the freedom of oneself and apply force to perform duties that aren't in your will. Taking full control of your mind now gives you all the power and authority to regulate what flows in and out and opens the door for seeds to be planted in your mind. This is something that you have to prioritize if freedom is something that you are interested in.

COMPARISON HAS NO WORTH / COMPARISON KILLS!

Comparing ourselves to others has by far been the most common starter for weak minds in our generation. In the world that we are living in today, social media has made it easy for individuals to hide their true identities through anonymity and has masked people with unnecessary expectations. Take a quick look at your hands. Are they the same? That's exactly how human beings are. We were all created differently and given different gifts and talents. Our experiences will also never be the same. So why compare yourself to someone on the internet? Who knows, you might not ever meet the person. Comparison brings jealousy, low self-esteem and can potentially lead to depression. There is absolutely no value in wasting your time and energy on other people's lives. Invest that time in getting to know yourself more, treating yourself, and discovering what your unique gifts are. When you repetitively compare yourself to others, you'll never get to enjoy the pleasure that comes with loving you.

DO NOT BE IGNORANT!

Ignorance simply means the lack of knowledge and understanding. It saddens me to know that our generation has settled and is trying to normalize ignorance. Where adults are acting and speaking like children and it's ignored. The sad truth is that people that you are surrounded by are people who are not eager to educate themselves on the importance of freedom and peace in your mind. So instead of them feeding you with positivity they rather add more fuel to your flame of fear. It's important to continuously educate yourself on fear and other related issues that cause setbacks in life and surround yourself with people who push you to get further in life and force you to face your fears.

The only way to run away from ignorance is to apply wisdom. Unfortunately, many people think that posting inspirational quotes on Instagram makes you wise. Wisdom can only be acquired through experience so if you fail to go through the storms that life throws at you, you are cheating yourself of the knowledge in the storm. Stay educated, go through things for yourself and apply the lessons that you learn from your experiences to your life, and I promise you that you will live a more fulfilled life.

"Ignorance isn't an excuse to make unwise decisions."
— Prince Aryee

SHIFT YOUR FOCUS

"A focused mind accomplishes."
— Prince Aryee

As a young adult, it is important to shift your focus from things you fear, things that terrify you and things that lead you into the tunnel of unwholesome thoughts to things that you are most grateful for, things that bring out the best in you and things that reflect the King and Queen that you are!

One mistake that most of us make is that we choose to walk on a path but in the process, we realize that it's not leading us to where we want to be in the future. Yet still, we keep walking down that wrong path hoping and believing that we can still breakthrough. Your life is a journey that requires a lot of attention, dedication, and time. Stop dwelling on your past and focus on where you are going. At one point in my life, I went through a season where I felt misunderstood. People that I thought were for me turned their backs against me because of a mistake I made. I went through a phase of self-judgment and I looked down on myself so much simply because my mind couldn't fathom everything that was said about me. But when I took the bold step of looking at myself in the mirror that God sees me in. Which is the mirror of love and compassion, I rose on my feet, faced it, and took back the keys that the enemy stole from me.

In my case, it was my joy, my happiness, and peace of mind. Once again you have a choice to make, you can either stay down and accept defeat or you can make up your mind that winning is the only option you have. Going through that made me stronger, wiser and shifted my focus to things of value. On

February 5, 2021, at 2:17 pm I wrote:

"Everyone makes mistakes in life. We say things and do things out of hurt, anger, past experiences, and all kinds of negative emotions.

Perhaps if I made different choices, I wouldn't be in the position that I'm in currently. Sometimes good people make bad choices. It doesn't mean they're bad.
It means they're human."

Don't allow your mistakes to move you away from destiny. Keep pressing on, the world needs your gift.

"Have you ever wondered why you always set goals but never accomplish them? It's simply because the lenses of your future have been distorted by the things that aren't worthy enough to be there."

– Prince Aryee

Shift Your Focus!

CHANGE YOUR ENVIRONMENT!

Changing your surroundings is crucial to the overall growth of your mind, especially after shifting your focus. Many people aspire to be the smartest individual in every room. But what you don't realize is that you end up placing a huge limit on your mind when you fail to surround yourself with people who are more knowledgeable than you simply because you are not being challenged to push yourself to exceed your current capacity.

I found myself wondering why certain people who I

considered close friends failed to understand things that I wanted to do and achieve in life. Some thought that my goals weren't realistic or achievable. After questioning myself numerous times, I came to the realization that It's not theirs to understand mainly because God didn't place the ideas and goals in their hearts, he placed and trusted it in mine. I immediately removed all these negative-minded people from my life and surrounded myself with people who are driven, goal oriented and people who are more aligned with the direction and path that I was taking.

One thing that I've realized in our generation is that removing negative people from our circle is a challenge. But also remember that "if it ain't for you, it's against you". Our day-to-day decisions are highly influenced by who and what we choose to surround ourselves with. Holding on to negative people is the first step to living an unfulfilled life. When that happens, positive things will be out of reach. The right choices are hindered by distractions. Many at times we expect people to help us bring our visions to life but one thing we have to keep in mind is that a man who doesn't see your future can't work as hard as you. Surround yourself with people who inspire you, challenge you and push you to do things that aren't in your comfort zone. Because "life begins at the end of your comfort zone".

Don't Give Up!

You can never know what your maximum capacity is if you stop at your weakest point.

ERASE GUILT

Guilt is the feeling you get when you believe in your heart or it is perceived that you have done something wrong. This mind-poisoning disease can also be generated through people around you. In my years of living, I've realized that guilt works in two ways. It either makes you weak until you can't do anything anymore or it empowers you to control and push harder in life than you already are. Luckily, I have experienced both of these impacts. It took me a long time to understand that guilt and shame is something that I don't have to deal with anymore mainly because Jesus carried all that weight when He died on the cross. But also, because the past can't be changed so the only thing that can be done is place focus on the future and how-to walk-in life without making those same mistakes that led to this undesirable feeling. In the process of healing, you will face this challenge multiple times but always remind yourself that no amount of guilt can change the past. Sometimes God takes you through the process of re-moulding. As a young adult myself, one thing we tend to do is look at the negative aspects of things so much that we lose focus of the blessing that is hidden in the storm. Wherever there is chaos, there is also a place of peace that is seeking to be discovered. In good or bad, look for the message life is giving you.

"If it's out of your hands, it deserves freedom from your mind too"
– Homebody Club

SHIFT THE BLAME!

Blaming someone or something for your failures has become a well-known remedy for making yourself feel better. When in reality, your poor choice of decisions caused you to fail or be unsuccessful. I'm not saying this to make you feel bad. I'm saying this to make you think and reflect on the number of times that you blamed people or objects for the bad things that happened in your life, knowing that you could've made one decision which would've changed the whole narrative of the situation.

"Only mature people own up to their faults and accept the consequences of their actions."
– Prince Aryee

No wonder I see and hear so many people shift the blame for the smallest things. As a young adult you have to be very alert because you can easily be a victim of their manipulation. It could be a family member, co-worker, boyfriend/girlfriend, husband/wife and even your parents. Many people's minds have been tuned to accept and believe false information that has shaped them to believe that they aren't who they think they are. If you are a victim of this, wake up and take charge of your life. Take the time to figure out who you really are because, *"if you don't know who you are and your identity, anybody can tell you who you are and you will believe it"* – **Samuel Amankwah.**

DO NOT WASTE TIME!

"If tomorrow isn't guaranteed
to you, then why waste today?"
– Prince Aryee

We are all at fault when this topic comes up. There have been times in your life where you knew you should've been doing something, but you kept procrastinating and pushing it away thinking that the desire will last forever. Once again, we are all at fault, including myself. "Time waits for no man" is a saying that I've heard over and over again, but I never understood it as a child until I realized how valuable time is.

When fear and anxiety creep up on you, it doesn't ask you if you are ready for it or not. It comes whenever it wants and in whatever way it wants. Now my question to you is, "Why are you waiting for the right time to face your fears knowing very well that fear disrespectfully stole your joy and your freedom from you?"

Completely put aside how long it will take to overcome the enemy because whether you like it or not time will pass by. The sad thing about failing to take action today is that all the time you wasted, you could've used that to take charge of your life again. Just start, just take that baby step, just walk towards the light and I promise you that it will be the best decision that you've ever made. Take the step because "If tomorrow isn't guaranteed to you, then why waste today?"

LET IT GO!

This title always brings me back to the story of Lot and his wife in the bible. Lot's wife was a woman who decided to disobey God's command and as a consequence she turned into a pilar of salt all because she looked back to see how Sodom and Gomorrah were getting destroyed. Her story always reminds me of things that can possibly happen to people who always look back and I personally use that as a guide to not cave into the things of the world but rather press on towards Jesus.

"Holding on to the past poisons what is ahead of you unknowingly."
– Prince Aryee

Why are you holding on to the past?

The fact that you are moving forward alone is a sign for you to not look back. You will miss people, things, experiences you had and many more but always remember that the memories ahead of you will be more valuable once you let the things of the past go. I've been in a position where I thought that I couldn't do something simply because I started the journey with someone, and it didn't feel right going on without the person. We've all been there but one thing you need to keep in mind is that whenever you look back, you are at risk of being stuck in your current circumstance. It can be friendships, relationships, jobs and even family, you always have to keep in mind that the only way you can figure out if you're going to be successful or not is if you step into the adventure yourself. Keep moving forward.

"You can spend minutes, hours, days, weeks, or even months over-analyzing a situation; trying to put the pieces together, justifying what could've, would've happened...or you can just leave the pieces on the floor and move on"

– Tupac Shakur

The reason why many young adults struggle with fear is because they are ready to progress and blossom into the next big things, but they aren't ready to let go of the things that are holding them back from achieving the next big thing. My challenge to you is to respect yourself enough to walk away from things that hold you back and create an environment that is conducive to your success.

TAKE THE TIME TO KNOW WHO YOU ARE!

Knowing who you are is the first step you need to take to be a victorious warrior in any battle you find yourself in. The only way you can know what you are capable of is by pushing yourself out of your comfort zone. Many people think that they know themselves, but they are being dragged along like dogs by social media, friends and things that aren't of great value.

Not taking time to know yourself opens the door for anyone to tell you who you are and what you are capable of. A person who knows him or herself will refuse

to accept things that people say
about them. It is quite
unfortunate that many people
have been paralyzed by what their
parents, peers and loved ones
have said about them. Many
parents have proclaimed negative
statements such as "you are
useless", "you are ugly", "you
will never make it in life", "your
goals are unrealistic" and many
more to their children at a very
young age which has now pushed
them to idolize people and things
on the internet and has shaped
the minds of individuals to
believe that they can never
achieve anything. But today is the
day that you will receive your
total freedom because you are
more than capable of doing

anything that you put your mind to.

It all starts by knowing who you are. So today my challenge to you is to spend time with yourself. Be curious and discover new things about yourself, new strengths, new talents and new gifts that you didn't know you had. I promise you; you will not regret this decision.

"You gain strength, courage and confidence by every experience in which you really stop to look fear in the face. You must do the things you think you cannot do"
— Eleanor Roosevelt

WHAT HAVE YOU LEARNED FROM THIS CHAPTER?

WHAT STEPS ARE YOU GOING TO TAKE TO BENEFIT FROM THE LESSON IN THIS CHAPTER?

CHAPTER THREE

MAINTING YOUR NEW TITLE AS A THE FEARLESS WARRIOR

(How To Navigate Through Life After Defeating Fear)

STOP RESPONDING

It's one thing to overcome fear but maintaining your freedom after that experience is another task that you have to prioritize. Always keep in mind that fear starts off by opening up a dialogue with your mind. The moment you respond to the language spoken to you; you set the tone for FEAR to speak directly to your mind.

"What conversation are you responding to?"

Fear and doubts will always come but it's up to you to decide if you are going to allow them to control your life. It's easy to go around holding on to mistakes that you have made, failures that you have seen and so many other things that weigh you down. It's time to let them go because the longer you keep them, the more receptive you will become. There is nothing more dangerous than knowing what the best thing to do is but not having the power to do so. Train your mind to only respond to positive things. Doing so wouldn't be easy but with the right push and determination, you can achieve this goal.

Behind fear is darkness but light is the only thing that shines the brightest through darkness.

Say this out loud.

I (Name)
I'm letting go of all the things that speak negativity into my life
I am taking full control of my life
Nothing on earth will stop me from achieving greatness
And I will be the light in every dark room

*"No response is a response. And it's a powerful one.
Remember that."
– Unknown*

FAITH OVER FEAR

As mentioned in the very first chapter of this book, Fear to me is simply a mental state of uncertainty with a hint of danger and anxiety. Fear comes in different shapes and forms especially when you become an adult. Some can destroy you and hurt everyone around you. Others, on the other hand, can just shape you to be more conservative. Faith in me is fully trusting in someone or something. As a Christian, I've come to the realization that putting my faith in God has changed and turned so many things which could've been negative into positives.

*"The Lord Himself goes before you
and will be with you. He will never
leave you nor forsake you. Do not be
afraid; do not be discouraged"*
– Deuteronomy 31:8

Having this in mind, I
confidently move forward and
face all my fears day by day
knowing that God will never
leave me nor forsake me. Now
my question to you is "Who or
what are you putting your trust
in? Family, friends, co-workers,
boyfriend or girlfriend?". It is
important to have an
understanding of who or what
you are trusting in and how your
life can be positively or negatively
shaped. Having faith that you are

going to overcome obstacles is a choice that you have to make and who you choose to put your trust in can determine your rate of success or failure.

"Faith and fear both demand you to believe in something you cannot see. You get to choose."
– Bob Proctor

EXPERIENCE THINGS FOR YOURSELF

"How many times have you stopped yourself from making a move or taking a step because of the results someone else got when they made that same move?"

I know we have all been victims of this where we don't take a step or make a move because of the results someone else got when they took that same step or made that same move.

The only question I have for you is
"Whose life story are you living?"

We often make the mistake of not going after our dreams and aspirations because fear has once again worked its way into our lives through available sources which can be your family, friends, business partners, spouse or even someone that you randomly met on the street. Experiencing things for yourself is the first step to building resilience. Resilience in simple terms is the ability to quickly recover from negative situations. The chances of you succeeding the first time you try something new is very low. That's just the truth. I know it's a hard pill to swallow but be real with yourself and don't set dreamlike expectations.

"When a man really desires something so deeply that he is willing to stake his entire future on a single turn of the wheel in order to get it, he is sure to win"
– Thomas Edison

CLEAR THE CLUTTER

Your mind is the most powerful part of your entire body. What you feed will determine how far you will go in life. You can either feed your mind with positive meals or negative meals. Unfortunately, those are the only options you have on this menu.

You have been treating your mind like a trash can and you expect it to have the scent of a rose plantation. Unfortunately, I don't feel bad for being real. Your mind is farmland. Planting bitterness, anger and unwholesome thoughts will force it to bear fruits like failure, disappointment and shame. Feeding it with positive affirmations and watering it with love on the other hand, will force it to grow and bear fruits like success, independence and self-worth. It's not too late to open up for fresh air to come into your mind.

Clear every undesirable thought out of your head and fill up your mind with things that will stimulate growth in your life.

LOVE YOURSELF

You have probably heard this numerous times, but the phrase "love yourself" has a deeper meaning than it sounds. Loving yourself paves the way for you to go through the most difficult situations with compassion knowing that no matter what happens you will always have your own back.

"What version of yourself are you believing?"

Every single person you come across in life has their own version of you in their heads and believing what they say about you can be easily implemented if you don't take the time to know and love yourself.

- Loving yourself makes it easier for you to say "no" to fear and pushes you to block out anybody or anything that triggers fear in your life.

- Loving yourself stops you from seeking approval from friends, family members and social media "influencers".

- Loving yourself enables you to take charge of your life. You get to decide on when and how you approach situations and how you want to live your life.

- Loving yourself finally opens the door for you to genuinely love others.

"How you love yourself is how you teach others to love you"
– Rupi Kaur

WHAT HAVE YOU LEARNED FROM THIS CHAPTER?

_____

_____

_____

_____

_____

_____

_____

_____

WHAT STEPS ARE YOU GOING TO TAKE TO BENEFIT FROM THE LESSON IN THIS CHAPTER?

_____

_____

_____

_____

_____

_____

_____

_____

"Courage doesn't mean you don't get afraid. Courage means you don't let fear stop you"
- Unknown

PRAYER

Good, Good Father,

I thank you for my life
I thank you for finding me
worthy to see another day
I thank you for your consistency
in my life

For if it had not been you God
on my side, where would I be
I started this journey with you,
and you stayed in the center of it
all
I thank you for that

As I'm going on in life with a
renewed mind
I'm asking you to fill me up with
power and never let your
presence depart from me
In Jesus Name

Amen!

ABOUT THE AUTHOR

Prince Aryee is the author of Overcoming Fear: An Essential Guide for The Audacious Young Adult. A Universal Banker and motivator by day and a fashion influencer by night. He was born in Ghana, West Africa and has lived most of his life in Brampton, Ontario. He studied Business Administration/Marketing at Humber College Institute of Advanced Learning and Technology. Prince always makes it a point to look, smell and most importantly feel his best whenever he steps out and his love for helping people is exhibited whenever and wherever he goes. He inspires and empowers people to defeat fear with his life experiences and consistently checks on the wellbeing of people around him.

You can chat with Prince on Instagram at @iampvince or check out his website at www.princearyee.com

Made in the USA
Monee, IL
20 May 2021

69131869R00059